Rottweiler puppy owned by Robert Sarro. Photo by Isabelle Français.

KW-229
Breeding Rottweilers

BREEDING ROTTWEILERS

Victoria L. Robertson

Title page: Rottweiler owned by David Lauster. Photo by I. Français.

Distributed in the UNITED STATES by T.F.H. Publications, Inc., One T.F.H. Plaza, Neptune City, NJ 07753; in CANADA to the Pet Trade by H & L Pet Supplies Inc., 27 Kingston Crescent, Kitchener, Ontario N2B 2T6; Rolf C. Hagen Ltd., 3225 Sartelon Street, Montreal 382 Quebec; in CANADA to the Book Trade by Macmillan of Canada (A Division of Canada Publishing Corporation), 164 Commander Boulevard, Agincourt, Ontario M1S 3C7; in ENGLAND by T.F.H. Publications, PO Box 15, Waterlooville PO7 6BQ; in AUSTRALIA AND THE SOUTH PACIFIC by T.F.H. (Australia) Pty. Ltd., Box 149, Brookvale 2100 N.S.W., Australia; in NEW ZEALAND by Ross Haines & Son, Ltd., 82 D Elizabeth Knox Place, Panmure, Auckland, New Zealand; in the PHILIPPINES by Bio-Research, 5 Lippay Street, San Lorenzo Village, Makati, Rizal; in SOUTH AFRICA by Multipet Pty. Ltd., P.O. Box 35347, Northway, 4065, South Africa. Published by T.F.H. Publications, Inc. Manufactured in the United States of America by T.F.H. Publications, Inc.

To my husband, Herb.

Rottweiler pups owned by Robert Sarro. Photo by I. Français.

"Newspapers are to breeders as diapers are to newborn parents, they both get a little bit nervous when the supply begins to dwindle."

Vicky Robertson

CONTENTS

The Rottweiler needs breeders who are dedicated to quality.

FOREWORD

I was very proud when asked to write the foreword for this book. It is important for new, young, energetic writers to get involved with supplying information to the new owner as well as to the breeders who have been around for awhile.

It takes time and patience to contact the breeders and sift through the tons of old tried-and-true methods and the new and wonderful methods of breeding, caring for your dog, and other aspects of ownership, then to put it down on paper to make it interesting to both the newcomer and old-timer alike.

Everyone needs to know what special problems their breed has and how to cope with them. What better place to get the answers than from the breeders of these animals.

Not only the new owner but even the old breeder, like myself, can get new ideas on how to handle a situation not usually covered in the other books or something they have not experienced in their everyday practice.

After 35 years I thought I had experienced everything, but everyday there is something new and mind-boggling to contend with.

Good luck, Vicky, in your quest for knowledge and your patience with the breeders, like myself, who will be only too happy to impress you with their wonderful dog stories and ways to cut costs.

HELEN DAVIS JONES
X-Cell's Kennels

Among the working breeds and protection dogs, the Rottweiler may be both the most handsome and most effective. No wonder dedicated breeders commit themselves to the betterment of these marvelous animals. Photo by I. Français.

PREFACE

I would like to take this time to thank everyone who helped put this book together.

A special thanks to Helen Davis Jones, a top breeder and my mother-in-law, who taught me everything I know about breeding. Most, but not all of the tips in this book were basic knowledge handed down from her.

Donna LaQuatra, a top Rottweiler breeder in the nation, also contributed her knowledge and tips for successful breeding.

Working on this book gave me the opportunity to learn a great deal about Rottweiler history and the splendid pedigrees of the great ancestors, the backbone of this breed.

It is exciting for any Rottie owner to discover that he/she owns a pup that came from a long line of international and famous champions known throughout the entire world of dogs. The power is then in that owner's hands to produce a litter worthy of that dog's heritage and to carry on the family name.

Breeding is not just getting puppies but the excitement of producing that perfect dog, the dog that outshines all others in the show ring, matches and exceeds the standard of its breed, and goes on winning for years and years.

Many breeders go on endlessly hoping to produce those perfect dogs while others, like Helen and Donna, have achieved those dreams and made them a reality.

I would like also to acknowledge Shane Henry, D.V.M., and authors Delbert G. Carlson, D.V.M., James M Giffin, M.D., *Dog Owner's Home Veterinary Handbook;* Phyllis A. Holst, D.V.M., *Canine Reproduction: A Breeders Guide;* and Richard Stratton, *The Rottweiler.*

INTRODUCTION

When it comes to reality, you can throw all those simple step-by-step whelping directions out the window: whelping does not go exactly as planned, and it never goes as easily and as matter-of-factly as the veterinary manuals predict. Every dog is different and every bitch is different. Of course, knowing the basics beforehand is an essential foundation on which to build your experience. These basics prove especially important in an emergency, such as when the mother does not remove the sac, does not deliver in a given number of hours, or develops eclampsia or a uterine infection. In such cases it is vital to know what to look for and how to

Rottweilers have big-litter demands. Here eight littermates vie for the nipples. This is X-Cell's Tuff Stuff owned by author Victoria Robertson.

The miracle of motherhood—caring for her offspring comes naturally to the dam.

act—you may save the animal's life.

The goal of this book is to slice through the accumulated, relentlessly specific data and to provide a clear and concise portrait of breeding a champion Rottweiler. Naturally, the specifics of various complications will be discussed, and an outline of proper procedures will be given; however, the information contained herein is designed to give the reader a broad perspective of the entire process and thereby enable him/her to achieve success in a breeding program.

Before we begin our journey, I would like to share an experience. Before the birth of my first Rottweiler puppies, I studied a manual on "When to Call the Vet and How to

Help a Puppy Breathe." I did not have to call the vet, but I did have to help a puppy breathe. The first ten puppies did fine without my services, but the next three did not—they all were born at the same time. The eleventh pup survived only because I had read that manual before and had some idea of what to do.

The mother was tired after ten puppies and did not even bother looking at the trio. I grabbed one and gave one to the mother, who started working on it while I worked on mine. After removing the sac, I

Invariably a special bond develops between puppy and child.

Young pups are delicate creatures that require special care and plenty of warmth and love. Photo by V. Serbin.

found the puppy's mouth and nose full of mucus. I used the "sling-the-puppy" method to revive him. I was afraid that it was not going to work because, after doing it three times, mucus was still coming out of his nose, but I kept on slinging.

Rubbing the sides of a pup back and forth and up and down usually works to start a puppy's breathing.

This time it did not. So I put him on my knees and puffed ever so gently into his mouth. He coughed. I continued. Two more times I puffed and he responded with coughing. I then gave him to his mother to be nurtured, hoping that he would survive, and he did.

This story exemplifies several important facts about breeding. First,

While their cuteness and cuddliness can be compared to that of any stuffed animal, puppies are living individuals who depend on us for their complete well-being.

problems do arise, often unexpectedly. The bitch was doing fine and all seemed well until....
Second, it pays to be prepared: had this author not read the manual and not been in a constant state of alertness, the pups might have been lost. Lastly, while many fine manuals are available, most are so specific or vast that to read them all would require more time than most of us have. Hence, the purpose of this book: to provide in an easy-to-read, straightforward manner the information necessary to meet the demands and achieve the goals set forth by responsible Rottweiler breeders.

Far too many puppies spend their last days viewing life from behind the confines of a shelter. Every breeder must take absolute responsibility for each pup he brings into this world.

THE CHAMPION ROTTWEILER

A champion Rottweiler possesses the title as well as the near-perfect conformation to the breed standard. Breeding the correct qualities is the first step in creating a champion, but selecting the two ideal mates is not easy—one breeder reviewed over 100 studs before picking the father of her complete champion litter (one pup from which went on to become No. 5 in the nation).

Champion traits to a large degree come from two parents that complement each other perfectly, a strength for a weakness and vice versa. Breeding is therefore a major part in the creation of a champion, but it is only a stepping stone to success. Once a pup is born with the qualities of excellence as specified by

All puppies should receive basic obedience training, for breeding and upbringing combine to make the champion.

The attractive Peltcs' Rm'd and Dangerous, T.T., taking Reserve. Breeder-owner, Cathleen Peltcs Crum. Photo by Earl Graham Studios.

the breed standard, the process has only begun.

To receive a championship title, a dog must compete in point shows, and these shows have become very populated with Rottweilers today. Points are awarded towards a championship title for placing first in the breed, with the championship points awarded determined by the number of dogs and bitches entered in the class in relation to the minimum number of entries required. All dogs are judged against the breed standard. Competition is stiff. With many popular shows recording 100–200 Rottweilers in attendance, attaining a championship title today is difficult and challenging. With these facts stated, it becomes clear that breeding the best possible Rottweiler is an imperative step in the achievement of eventual success: to attain a championship is to "create" a champion. You, the breeder, have the choice of whelping a litter of champions or of run-of-the-mill dogs.

Unfortunately, "trash" is infiltrating today's Rottweiler breed. Money-minded breeders are mating any Rottweiler that they get their hands on for the simple purpose of producing a litter, and the breed as a whole is weakened by such practice. Rottweilers are emerging with small, thin, poorly muscled bodies;

Breed only if there is a great likelihood of the offspring's achieving near-ideal conformation to the breed standard. Photo by I. Francais, courtesy of handler Nancy Hapward.

Rottweilers are very intelligent, very trainable animals who always strive to do better. Here a Rottweiler gracefully clears three boards in the high jump.

small, pencil-thin heads; and close-set beady eyes. These are traits that no Rottweiler should possess.

Some misinformed or ill-intentioned people are breeding half-Rottweilers with half-Doberman/half-Rottweilers, thinking that eventually they create whole-Rottweilers! Such breedings will never produce a Rottweiler. All that they can possibly create is a big mess, as other misinformed people buy these puppies without papers thinking that the dogs are purebreds (because that is what the breeder told them). They then breed to other Rottweilers, thus creating even more pups that are pawned off as purebreds without papers. One thing is certain: if the dog does not have papers and the owner does not know the pedigree, there is a good possibility that the dog is not pure and the animal should not be purchased—and especially should not be bred as a purebred. A word of caution: be careful! Some breeders even

temperament, and proper age range.

PRELIMINARY CONCERNS

Breeding is a challenging, self-gratifying sport, hobby or profession in which the participant can help to

produce or purchase fake papers. Breed only with dogs from reputable breeders, champions or potential champions. Potential champion means very good pedigree, close conformation to the standard, even

Only by following sound breeding practices can a breeder give his pups a fair start in life.

create and nurture the future of the breed. Many breeders do not understand the importance

Breeders must select for temperament as carefully as they select for physical characteristics. Photo by R. Reagan of Rottie bred and owned by Ron Gibson.

of sound breeding practices. The fact is that today's puppies are tomorrow's leaders or losers, depending on their quality and ability. Therefore, novices need to study the breed before attempting to breed, and professionals need to be even more selective.

What makes Rottweilers unique and so popular is their special personality and characteristics. The Rottweiler is an intelligent breed with ominous protection performance, complete loyalty and compassion for its master, and a continuous urge to please. The dog's appearance is bold, striking, powerful and fearless. People are overwhelmed by the aura of power and dignity and the ability to instill fear in a stranger yet be cuddly like a teddy bear to his owner. "A face only a mother could love,"

strangers often remark at first impression.

The satisfaction derived from breeding these animals is immense. However, there are precautions to take with this breed. It must be understood by the buyer that the dog's power and strength, although perhaps

The new owner may not fully realize how big and powerful these innocent little creatures become—and breeders must educate all newcomers to the breed.

the most notable aspects of the breed, can also be drawbacks. The Rottweiler naturally protects and can attack an unintroduced stranger if left alone with him. The dog can also mistake a friendly visitor as a trespasser and, because

Naturally protective, Rottweilers excel at guard-dog training. However, the dog's instincts must be carefully channeled, and the learned-responses, tightly controlled.

of its natural protection instincts, attack without true warrant. It is the obligation of the owner to understand this protective instinct and tactfully introduce all visitors to the dog. Do this by touching the person (this shows the dog that the person can be trusted),

Early socializing of Rottweiler puppies reinforces the canine natural love and respect of man. Socializing is fundamental in raising of any normal, well-balanced dog.

announce the name, then touch the dog with words of approval.

The attack instinct in the Rottweiler is the most distinctive and, in the opinion of the author, probably the main reason why the dog is so popular. It is a very dependable breed for protection purposes; but, like a loaded gun in the wrong hands, the Rottweiler can be misused. Normally, a family dog will never attack the family or children. My kids grew up rolling all over three large Rottweilers, pulling at their ears, jumping on their backs, etc. The dogs would never harm the children. If the dog is well bred, the temperament of the Rottie is sweet, gentle, and, of course, cuddly. The problem today is that most inexperienced breeders do not understand the importance of quality breeding, especially where temperament is concerned. In dogs this large and powerful, temperament should be the first issue.

PORTRAITS OF THE IDEAL ROTTWEILER

ORIGINAL GERMAN STANDARD FOR THE ROTTWEILER

Appearance: A good-sized, strong, muscular well-built dog with intelligence and extreme loyalty.

Head: The skull is broad between the ears, stop well pronounced, short muzzle. Well-developed nose with large nostrils and should be black. Strong muscular jaws, well-pronounced, strong teeth, incisors of

Barker's Alexis Vom Lenhart, owned by Donna LaQuatra, taking Winners at the Tampa Bay Kennel Club show. Photo by Earl Graham Studios.

lower jaw must touch the inner surface of the upper incisors. Eyes are of medium size, dark brown, which express loyalty and confidence. The ears

Headstudy of Ch. Arcturus Von Ross, a linebred great grandson of the famous German Ch. Dux Vom Hungerbuhl. He is rated O.F.A. Excellent.

should be small, set high and wide and hang over about on a level with top of head. The skin on the head should be firm. The neck should be strong, round and very muscular.

Forequarters: Shoulders should be well placed, long and sloping, elbows well let down. Legs muscular with plenty of substance. Feet should be round, toes well arched, soles very hard, toenails dark, strong and short.

Body: The chest is large, broad and vast. Ribs well sprung. Back straight, strong and short. Croup short, broad but not sloping.

Hindquarters: Upper thighs should be short, wide and very muscular. Lower thigh should be very muscular at the top and

Loved by many, feared by some, respected by all! Photo by I. Francais.

strong and shaped at the bottom. Stifles fairly well bent, hocks strong. The hind feet are longer than the front but should be close and strong with toes well arched. No dewclaws.

Tail: Should be short, high (on level with back). Dogs are born with a short stump tail, but if they are not, the tail should be docked close to the body.

Coat: Hair should be coarse, short and flat. The undercoat which is required on neck and thighs should not show through the outer coat.

Color: Black, clearly defined markings on cheeks, muzzle, chest and

Schaden's Won N Only Von Ursa, owned by Cathleen A. Crum, displays her conformation to the breed standard. Photo by Earl Graham Studios.

BeaBear's Solid as a Rock, owned by Sandy Buczkowski and Donna LaQuatra, taking B.O.S. from the American-bred Class under judge E. Frese.

legs as well as over both eyes. Color of markings— tan or mahogany brown. Spots of white on the chest and belly are not desirable but are permissible.

Height: Shoulder height for males is 23¼-27 inches (58–69 cm); for females, 21 ¾–25¾ inches (53–64 cm). Height should always be considered in relation to the appearance and conformation of the dog.

Faults: Too lightly built or too heavily built. Sway back. Body too long. Head too long and narrow or too short and plump. Snipy muzzle, floppy cheeks, line of muzzle not straight, light or flesh-colored nose. Hanging flews. Overshot or undershot jaw. Loose skin on head. Ears set too low or too heavy. Long or narrow ears or ears of uneven lengths. Light, small or slanting eyes. Neck too long, thin or weak or too much throatiness. Lack of bone and muscle. Short or straight shoulders. Front legs too close together or not straight. Weak pasterns, splay feet, weak toes, flat ribs, sloping croup. Too heavy or plump body. Flat thighs, cowhocks or weak hocks. Dewclaws. Tail set too high or too low or one that is too long or too thin. Soft, too short, too long or too open coat. Wavy coat or lack of undercoat. White markings on toes, legs or other body parts. Markings not well defined, smudgy. The one-color tan Rottweiler with either black or light mask or with black streak on back as well as other colors such as brown or blue are not recognized

Ch. Beaverbrook's Meister Brau, owned by Donna LaQuatra, has attained both his American and Bahamian Championships.

THE WORLD'S LARGEST SELECTION OF PET AND ANIMAL BOOKS

T.F.H. Publications publishes more than 900 books covering many hobby aspects (dogs.

. . . BIRDS . .

. . CATS . . .

. . . ANIMALS . . .

. . . DOGS . .

cats, birds, fish, small animals, etc.), plus books dealing with more purely scientific aspects of the animal world (such as books about fossils, corals, sea shells, whales and octopuses). Whether you are a beginner or an advanced hobbyist you will find exactly what you're looking for among our complete listing of books. For a free catalog fill out the form on the other side of this page and mail it today. All T.F.H. books are recyclable.

. . FISH . . .

For many avid fanciers, show competition consummates their dedicated efforts. Photo by I. Francais.

and are believed to be crossbred, as is a longhaired Rottweiler. Timid or stupid-appearing animals are to be positively rejected.

OFFICIAL AMERICAN KENNEL CLUB STANDARD FOR THE ROTTWEILER

General Appearance: The ideal Rottweiler is a medium large, robust and powerful dog, black with clearly defined rust markings. His compact and substantial build denotes great strength, agility and endurance. Dogs are characteristically more massive throughout with larger frame and heavier bone than bitches. Bitches are distinctly feminine, but without weakness of substance or structure.

Size Proportion, Substance: Dogs—24 inches to 27 inches. Bitches—22 inches to 25 inches, with preferred size being mid-range of each sex. Correct proportion is of primary importance, as long as size is within the standard's range.

The length of the body, from prosternum to the rearmost projection of the rump, is slightly longer than the height of the dog at the withers, the most desirable proportion of the height to length being 9 to 10. The Rottweiler is neither coarse nor shelly. Depth of chest is approximately fifty percent (50%) of the height of the dog. His bone and muscle mass must be sufficient to balance his frame, giving a compact and very powerful appearance. *Serious Faults*—Lack of proportion, undersized, oversized, reversal of sex characteristics (bitchy dogs, doggy bitches).

Head: Of medium length, broad between the ears; forehead line seen in profile is moderately arched; zygomatic arch and stop well developed with strong broad upper and lower jaws. The desired ratio of backskull to muzzle is 3 to 2. Forehead is preferred dry, however some wrinkling may occur when dog is alert. *Expression* is noble, alert, and self-assured.

Eyes of medium size, almond shaped with well fitting lids, moderately deep-set, neither protruding nor receding. The desired color is a uniform dark brown. *Serious Faults*— Yellow (bird of prey) eyes, eyes of different color or size, hairless eye rim. *Disqualification*—Entropion. Ectropion.

Ears of medium size, pendant, triangular in shape; when carried alertly the ears are level with the top of the skull and appear to broaden it. Ears are to be set well apart, hanging

Facing page: *One of the majestic Rottweilers that appeared at the annual World Dog Show in Europe. Photo by I. Francais.*

forward with the inner edge lying tightly against the head and terminating at approximately mid-cheek. *Serious Faults*—Improper carriage (creased, folded or held away from cheek/head).

Muzzle—Bridge is straight, broad at base with slight tapering towards tip.

Your dog must accept handling and inspection of his mouth if he is to compete successfully.

The end of the muzzle is broad with well developed chin. Nose is broad rather than round and always black. Lips—Always black; corners closed; inner mouth pigment is preferred dark. *Serious Faults*—Total lack of mouth pigment (pink mouth).

Bite and Dentition—Teeth 42 in number (20 upper, 22 lower) strong, correctly placed, meeting in a scissors bite—lower incisors touching inside of upper incisors. *Serious Faults*—Level bite; any missing tooth. Disqualifications— Overshot, undershot (when incisors do not touch or mesh); wry mouth; two or more missing teeth.

Neck Topline, Body: Neck— Powerful, well muscled, moderately long, slightly arched and without loose skin. *Topline*—The back is firm and level, extending in a straight line from behind the withers to the croup. The back remains horizontal to the ground while the dog is moving or

Ch. Drauf Vom Mayerhof, affectionately known as Cannonball, taking B.O.S. owner-handled by Donna LaQuatra.

standing.

Body—The chest is roomy, broad and deep, reaching to elbow, with well pronounced forechest and well sprung, oval ribs. Back is straight and strong. Loin is short, deep and well muscled. Croup is broad, of medium length and only slightly sloping. Underline of a mature Rottweiler has a slight tuck-up. Males must have two normal testicles properly descended into the

The Rottweiler should possess a deep, broad, roomy chest and a straight, strong back. There should be a slight tuck-up to the underline of the mature Rottie. Photo by I. Francais.

scrotum. *Disqualification—* Unilateral cryptorchid or cryptorchid males.

Tail docked short, close to body, leaving one or two tail vertebrae. The set of the tail is more important than length. Properly set, it gives an impression of elongation of topline; carried slightly above horizontal when the dog is excited or moving.

Forequarters: Shoulder blade is long and well laid back. Upper arm equal in length to shoulder blade, set so elbows are well under body. Distance from withers to elbow and elbow to ground is equal. Legs are strongly developed with straight, heavy bone, not set close together. Pasterns

The standard for the Rottweiler breed is intended to describe a functionally capable dog as much as an esthetically pleasing animal.

The Rottweiler has been incorporated into the ranks of the military for the value of its physical and mental attributes. Photo by I. Francais.

are strong, springy and almost perpendicular to the ground. Feet are round, compact with well arched toes, turning neither in nor out. Pads are thick and hard. Nails short, strong and black. Dewclaws may be removed.

Hindquarters: Angulation of hindquarters balances that of forequarters. Upper thigh is fairly long, very broad and well muscled. Stifle joint is well turned.

Lower thigh is long, broad and powerful, with extensive muscling leading into a strong hock joint. Rear pasterns are nearly perpendicular to the ground. Viewed from the rear hind legs are straight, strong and wide enough apart to fit with a properly built body. Feet are somewhat longer than the front feet, turning neither in nor out, equally compact with well arched toes. Pads are thick and hard. Nails short, strong, and black. Dewclaws must be removed.

Coat: Outer coat is

straight, coarse, dense, of medium length and lying flat. Undercoat should be present on neck and thighs, but the amount is influenced by climatic conditions. Undercoat should not show through outer coat. The coat is shortest on head, ears and legs, longest on breeching. The Rottweiler is to be exhibited in the natural condition with no trimming. *Fault*—Wavy coat. *Serious Faults*—Open, excessively short, or curly coat; total lack of undercoat; any trimming that alters the length of the natural coat. *Disqualification*—Long coat.

Color: Always black with rust to mahogany markings. The demarcation between black and rust is to be clearly defined. The markings should be located as follows: a spot over each eye; on cheeks; as a strip around each side of muzzle, but not on the bridge of the nose; on throat; triangular mark on both sides of prosternum; on forelegs from carpus downward to the toes; on inside of rear legs showing down the front of the stifle and broadening out to front of rear legs from hock to toes, but not completely eliminating black from rear of pasterns; under tail; black penciling on toes. The undercoat is gray, tan, or black. Quantity and location of rust markings is important and should not exceed ten percent of body color. *Serious Faults*—Straw-colored, excessive, insufficient or sooty markings; rust marking other than described above; white marking any place on a dog (a few rust or white hairs do not constitute a marking). *Disqualifications*—Any base color other than black; absence of all markings.

Gait: The Rottweiler is a trotter. His movement should be balanced, harmonious, sure, powerful and unhindered, with strong forereach and a powerful rear drive. The motion is effortless, efficient, and ground-covering. Front and

Top and Bottom: *Truly the athletic animal, the Rottweiler combines great strength with excellent agility.*

rear legs are thrown neither in nor out, as the imprint of hind feet should touch that of forefeet. In a trot the forequarters and hindquarters are mutually coordinated while the back remains level, firm and relatively motionless. As with a wait-and-see attitude to influences in his environment. He has an inherent desire to protect home and family, and is an intelligent dog of extreme hardness and adaptability with a strong willingness to work, making him especially

speed increases the legs will converge under body towards a center line.

Temperament: The Rottweiler is basically a calm, confident and courageous dog with a self-assured aloofness that does not lend itself to immediate and indiscriminate friendships. A Rottweiler is self-confident and responds quietly and

With abundant endurance and a strong work ethic, the Rottweiler requires plenty of exercise to develop its finest qualities.

suited as a companion, guardian and general all-purpose dog.

The behavior of the Rottweiler in the show ring should be controlled, willing and adaptable, trained to submit to examination of mouth, testicles, etc. An aloof or reserved dog should not be penalized, as this reflects the accepted character of the breed. An aggressive or belligerent attitude towards other dogs should not be faulted.

A judge shall excuse from the ring any shy Rottweiler. A dog shall be judged fundamentally shy if, refusing to stand for examination, it shrinks away from the judge.

A dog that in the opinion of the judge menaces or threatens him/her, or exhibits any sign that it may not be safely approached or examined by the judge in the normal manner, shall be excused from the ring. A dog that in the opinion of the judge attacks any person in the ring shall be disqualified.

SUMMARY

Faults: The foregoing is a description of the ideal Rottweiler. Any structural fault that detracts from the above described working

The importance of temperament to the Rottweiler breed cannot be overstated. This Rottie is walking across a strange surface as part of its temperament test. Photo by R. Pearcy.

dog must be penalized to the extent of the deviation.

Disqualifications: Entropion, ectropion. Overshot, undershot (when incisors do not touch or

The Rottweiler must display a bold and courageous character, and never be shy or vicious. Photo by R. Pearcy.

mesh); wry mouth; two or more missing teeth. Unilateral cryptorchid or cryptorchid males. Long coat. Any base color other than black; absence of all markings. A dog that in the opinion of the judge attacks any person in the ring.

Approved May 8, 1990.

KENNEL CLUB OF GREAT BRITAIN STANDARD FOR THE ROTTWEILER

General Appearance: Above average size, stalwart dog. Correctly proportioned, compact and powerful form, permitting great strength, manoeuvrability and endurance.

Characteristics: Appearance displays boldness and courage. Self-assured and fearless. Calm gaze should indicate good humour.

Temperament: Good natured, not nervous, aggressive or vicious; courageous, biddable, with natural guarding instincts.

Head and Skull: Head medium length, skull broad between the ears. Forehead is moderately arched as seen from the side. Occipital bone well developed but not conspicuous. Cheeks well boned and muscled but not prominent. Skin on head not loose, although it may form a moderate wrinkle

Rottweilers in repose—still ever-alert and ready for action. Photo by R. Pearcy.

when attentive. Muzzle fairly deep with topline level, and length of muzzle in relation to distance from well defined stop to occiput, to be as 2 is to 3. Nose well developed with proportionally large nostrils, always black.

Eyes: Medium size, almond shaped, and dark brown in colour, light eye undesirable, eyelids close fitting.

Ears: Pendant, small in proportion rather than large, set high and wide apart on the head, lying flat and close to cheek.

Mouth: Teeth strong,

47

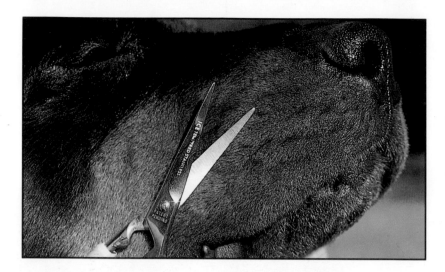

complete dentition with the scissors bite, i.e., upper teeth closely overlapping the lower teeth and set square to the jaws. Flews black and firm, falling gradually away towards corners of mouth, which do not protrude excessively.

Neck: Of fair length, strong, round and very muscular. Slightly arched, and free from throatiness.

Forequarters: The shoulders well laid back, long and sloping, elbows well let down, but not loose. Legs straight, muscular, with plenty of bone and substance. Pasterns

To accentuate the lines of the face and muzzle, many owners trim the whiskers. Photo by R. Reagan of Rottweiler owned by Ron Gibson.

sloping slightly forward.

Body: Chest roomy, broad and deep with well sprung ribs. Depth of brisket will not be more, and not much less than fifty percent of the shoulder height. Back straight, strong and not too long, ratio of shoulder height to length of body should be as 9 is to 10, loins short, strong and deep, flanks not tucked up. Croup of proportionate length, and broad, very slightly sloping.

Hindquarters: Upper thigh not too short, broad and strongly muscled. Lower thigh well muscled at top, strong and sinewy below. Stifles fairly well

Feet: Strong, round and compact with toes well arched. Hind feet somewhat longer than front. Pads very hard, toenails short, dark and strong. Rear dewclaws removed.

The Rottweiler's back should be straight and strong; when moving or standing the topline is level.

bent. Hocks well angulated without exaggeration, metatarsals not completely vertical. Strength and soundness of hock highly desirable.

Tail: Normally carried horizontally, but slightly above horizontal when dog is alert. Customarily docked at first joint, it is strong and not set too low.

Gait: Conveys an impression of supple strength, endurance and purpose. While back remains firm and stable, there is a powerful hindthrust and good stride. First and foremost, movement should be harmonious, positive and unrestricted.

Coat: Consists of top coat and undercoat. Top coat is of medium length, coarse and flat. Undercoat, essential on the neck and thighs, should not show through the top coat. Hair may also be a little longer on the back of the forelegs

The Rottweiler's forehead should be moderately arched as viewed from the side. Photo by I. Francais; agent, Steve Woj culewski.

The Rottweiler must have clearly defined markings, as is neatly spelled out in the breed standard. Photo by R. Pearcy.

and breechings. Long or excessively wavy coat highly undesirable.

Colour: Black with clearly defined markings as follows: a spot over each eye, on cheeks, as a strip around each side of muzzle, but not on bridge of nose, on throat, two clear triangles on either side of the breast bone, on forelegs from carpus downward to toes, on inside of rear legs from hock to toes, but not completely eliminating black from back of legs, under tail. Colour of markings from rich tan to mahogany and should not exceed ten percent of body colour. White marking is highly undesirable. Black pencil markings on toes are desirable. Undercoat is grey, fawn, or black.

Size: Dogs height at shoulder 63–69 cm (25–27 inches), bitches between 58–63.5 cm (23–25 inches). However, height should always be considered in relation to general appearance.

Note: Male animals should have two apparently normal testicles fully descended into the scrotum.

Faults: Any departure from the foregoing points should be considered a fault and the seriousness with which the fault should be regarded should be in exact proportion to its degree. The following faults are noted for the clarification of the standard: 1) Too lightly or too heavily built. 2) Sway backed or roach backed. 3) Cow hocked, bow hocked, or weak hocked. 4) Long or excessively wavy coat. 5) Any white markings. 6) Nervousness and viciousness are highly undesirable.

When assessing a dog's conformation, judges and owners alike must apply utmost objectivity.

Only by excellent breeding and rearing practices can one hope to achieve the potential offered in the Rottweiler breed. Photo by I. Francais of Rottie owned by Ann Wasserman.

THE BITCH

The excitement of breeding my Rottweiler bitch was beginning to disappear, and my previous enthusiasm was being replaced with dismay. The prospect of creating beautiful Rottweiler pups seemed great until she began her first season. Male dogs came out of the woodwork and everywhere else imaginable. I eventually was to meet what seemed like every male dog in the neighborhood. All, I might add, in hot pursuit.

Besides fighting off my Great Dane, which was a constant battle, every time I looked there was another dog in my backyard. They were jumping the four-foot fence with ease, squeezing through by the gate, and before it was over, even

Canines can have a hard time keeping cool when the heat of breeding season is on—sometimes a dip in the pool may help! Photo of Rottie owned by Donna LaQuatra.

digging under the fence.

One day a mixed Collie was in the yard. Early the next morning I awoke at 2 a.m. to find a black Lab making a narrow escape over the back fence. Later that day a German Shepherd, a mongrel, and a white shaggy "watchamacallit" all needed chasing away. The black Lab was more persistent than the others.

Late one night while I sat by my back door, I saw a shadow lurking. Tingles went up my spine. Boldly I moved my eyes in the direction of the shadow, while the rest of my body froze with fear. There, staring through the French windows of my back door was the menacing black Lab. Anxiety turned to anger, and I chased him off.

The game was getting quite annoying at this point. Three more dogs were chased off the next day; most did not return, but one always persisted. One night my husband decided that action was in order. With no

The parenting instinct is strong in most bitches, and some may "adopt" stuffed animals when they don't have a litter to care for.

shoes on and only a bathrobe flapping in the breeze, off he went in a frenzy, stick in hand, to chase the dog whose blackness blended with the darkness. He returned, burrs in his feet and scratches on his face, defeated only for the moment. He was determined to get that dog and put him where he belonged, wherever it might be. We never did catch the sly rascal. But we did succeed in producing Rottweiler pups after all!

Dogs have been known to jump through plate-glass windows to get to a bitch in season. They go mad by the scent that the female gives off, and they go to pieces if not allowed to catch her. Some males become so overcome with grief that they won't eat; they lie for days without

moving, howl uncontrollably, and run and pace back and forth until they lose as much as ten pounds. They will jump high fences with little regard to reprimand. They will become so crazed at times that sedation is very helpful to the owner's sanity

Socializing the puppies plays a vital role in the rearing of good pet Rottweilers. Rottie pups owned by Schwartz and Brechter photographed by Ron Reagan.

Donna LaQuatra demonstrates how good hard play helps our Rottweiler friends to expend their great energy.

(sedation of the animal, of course).

Preventing a cluster of males is not always easy, but it can be done by taking the bitch away in the car to relieve herself or by taking her to a kennel for a couple of weeks.

THE BITCH'S HEAT

To have a successful breeding you should have some idea of what is happening to the bitch during each stage of her season. This way you can mate her at the proper time without a lot of guesswork.

The beginning of the

bitch's season starts with the swelling of the vulva and a small amount of discharge. Following this is the period of time when the bitch will allow a male to mount her. This period lasts on the average from nine days to three weeks. The actual conception takes place approximately three days after ovulation. It is followed by a two-month period of pregnancy (58–63 days).

To know exactly when to mate the bitch, it is best to have your veterinarian do a "smear," as this will pinpoint the proper time. Rottweilers seem to have especially long seasons. They usually are not ready to mate until the middle or end of the second week (the 10th to 15th day).

Age is important. A

Preparation for breeding begins a good six to nine months before the actual mating so that, at the time of breeding, the bitch is in peak condition.

female over the age of six or seven is at risk when she becomes pregnant. The older the bitch, the more complications she tends to incur during pregnancy and delivery. If the bitch is in good physical condition and is not aging rapidly, she may breed without problems. First, she should

seasons should not be allowed to mate. It is too soon for her body to function properly and ensure herself and the pups a healthy life. Bitches that are allowed to breed in their first season, or before they are one-and-a-half years of age, very frequently have complications, often for life.

Create a checklist, and then start checking off—it's never too early to start preparing.

be checked by a vet to determine if she can handle the stress. A young bitch who has not yet had two

And, in many instances, the puppies die.

Fertilization does not occur until a couple of days after the mating. Therefore, it is very important to prevent any other male from coming into contact with the bitch until she is entirely out of season. It is

Even if the bitch mistakenly conceives during her first season, it may well be advised that the litter be carried and not aborted.

possible for a litter to be sired by more than one male because the sperm is held in storage by the female until conception occurs. If a second male is allowed to mount the already mated bitch, it is possible for pups of the same litter to be of different fathers. The offspring of a bitch bred in this manner are not accepted for registry by AKC and most other registries of dogs.

If a bitch somehow mates with a mongrel or a dog of another breed, it will not ruin her or her future litters. Most veterinarians suggest that you let her have the pups because it is safer than aborting them. Her future litters will depend on the future sire and not on previous matings.

ABORTION

Unless it is dangerous for the bitch to carry the puppies, most breeders and veterinarians prefer *not* to give an abortion, due to the risks.

There is an estrogen injection that can be used to abort an unwanted or dangerous pregnancy. However, the increased estrogen can cause changes in the uterus that can lead to pyometra (a diseased uterus).

An abortion will cause the bitch to remain in heat, or in season, for one or two weeks longer than usual, but it will also terminate the pregnancy. It is possible for the bitch to become pregnant again after an abortion, so she must be kept away from all males.

SEARCHING FOR A SIRE

When selecting a male, it is important to look at his pedigree. It is also important, however, to look at the dog himself. A long line of champions is usually—but not always—an indicator of quality puppies. Undesirable qualities sometimes appear, and if the dog shows evidence of poor quality, it will most likely show in the offspring.

Searching for a quality sire can be a very frustrating chore. To aid your quest, you should have the ideal Rottweiler etched in your mind and search for a male that best

There are many handsome males available for stud work, but good looks are only a small part of the picture. Photo by I. Francais of dog owned by Catherine Thompson.

represents that image. Viewing quality dogs often takes miles of driving. However, you can also visit AKC- and other kennel-club-sanctioned dog shows, where many fine dogs are often on display. There may be many fine Rottweilers at for the money. As he also suspected, many unhappy breeders are getting stuck with entire litters of poor-quality puppies, and the breed in general has suffered the consequences. In some areas, the breed is getting ruined by

these shows, but beware, for there are also a lot of dogs that you wouldn't want to breed to. The breed is being "sludged" by poor breeding, and the future of the breed is at stake because of it.

We must always consider the dog's ability to perform before breeding that animal.

Just as Richard Stratton predicted in his book *The Rottweiler*, too many people are breeding Rotties only

overbreeding of below-standard dogs, producing what one Rottie owner called, "houndy-looking things."

We owe it to the pups to follow only the most responsible breeding practices—they are totally dependent on their breeders for their care and placement into good homes.

Seeking out an excellent sire is important now more than ever. Mating prerequisites are easily overlooked by some, but they absolutely must not be if your goal is to produce sound, well-bred pups. Here are some mating prerequisites that should be kept in mind: work only with a reputable breeder; study thoroughly the coloring and other outstanding traits of both animals; check temperament; carefully note any and all faults (two dogs having the same fault or faults must not be bred—choose only a sire that complements the female's weaknesses and vice-versa); check that both dogs have a sound pedigree (meaning an overall healthy lineage) and no health related problems in their backgrounds; insist on an O.F.A. certification; if possible, investigate the entire line of the kennel; compare dominant traits; and, most importantly, breed to improve the breed and not just to get any old bunch of puppies.

A happy and free-wheeling Rottie. Veterinary technology today makes it absolutely unnecessary to breed any dog that is not free from the debilitating disease of hip dysplasia.

WHAT IS O.F.A.?

The Orthopedic Foundation for Animals based at the University of Missouri at Columbia established a voluntary program to evaluate radiographs of purebred dogs for evidence of hip dysplasia and other orthopedic problems. It charges a small fee and all films are reviewed by a panel of qualified veterinary radiologists. The organization returns a report to the owner of record and to the referring veterinarian. If the dog's X-rays prove normal for his breed, the dog will be certified with an O.F.A. number. The dog must be 24 months or older to receive O.F.A. certification. However, dogs of any age can be tested for the presence of this disease, though its absence cannot be confirmed until at least 24 months of age.

Applications for O.F.A. participation are acquired at most veterinarians'offices or by writing to: The

Orthopedic Foundation for Animals, Inc., University of Missouri-Columbia, Columbia, Missouri 65211. The O.F.A. may have temporarily saved the Rottweiler breed by helping most breeders use only

Again, breeders must be more careful now than ever before if the breed is to stay sound and beautiful.

AVOID BREEDING IF . . .
If you cannot breed to a dog as good as the one you

A successful tie: the bringing together of two carefully considered dogs.

certified dogs and bitches. However, other dangers linger, such as elbow dysplasia, retinal disorders, cataracts, and cancer.

have, do not breed. Never breed down, meaning never breed to a dog that has a substantial fault that your dog does not have. Doing so will only prolong the fault and create problems in the future.

Some dogs cannot be

bred because of specific defects or physical handicaps that will weaken the breed if passed on to their offspring. Do not breed any dog that is:

1. A male with only one testicle. He should be neutered. A dog like this is not eligible to compete in an AKC-sanctioned show.

2. Any dog with positive or severe hip dysplasia, elbow dysplasia, entropion, or a bad bite.

3. A bitch with mites or worms; all bitches should be wormed before mating since worms and mites could be passed on to the pups.

4. Any animal without all its shots; vaccinations should be up-to-date before any breeding takes place.

5. Any dog with any type of illness such as kennel cough, a virus, an infection, etc.

TYPES OF BREEDING

A breeder must determine desirable traits and choose a mate that enhances or establishes these traits. Unwanted or undesirable traits can be eliminated by special process breeding. Two popular processes used by experienced breeders are *linebreeding* and *inbreeding*.

Linebreeding is a process whereby dogs of fairly close relationship are bred together. Both dogs usually share a common ancestor, preferably from a second or third generation. (Sometimes a more distant relation is used, achieving satisfactory results.) This method is used most often by experienced breeders.

Inbreeding is the process whereby two closely related dogs, such as mother and son or sister and brother, are mated to concentrate desired traits. This type of mating is not advised

Facing page: *Ch. Arcturus Von Ross is a linebred great grandson of German Ch. Dux Vom Hungerbuhl, the top Rottweiler producer of his time.*

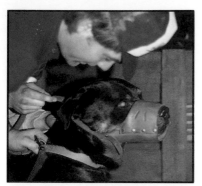

Here, Baron Von Wolfmeyer is muzzled as a precaution against injury to himself or the breeder. Owner: Bryan Huggins.

because of the uncertain results. More than half the resulting litter can be unsatisfactory, with only one or two quality pups born. Only experienced breeders who understand the genetic process should use this type of breeding.

MORE FACTS ABOUT MATING

Most males will take well to mating, while others just cannot get the hang of things. Sometimes it may be as simple as intimidation caused by a strange environment that causes the male not to perform. For this reason, the female is

ordinarily taken to the male, since the male tends to be more territorial.

When faced with an inexperienced stud, some breeders use artificial insemination. This can be done at the veterinarian's office. Others simply try to help the stud along. It is wise to protect yourself if you choose to go this route, because at this excited stage the male's or female's reaction is unpredictable. A leather muzzle should be placed over each dog's snout to prevent your being bitten.

If there is a problem concerning where to mate the two dogs (conditions are unfavorable at both homes), then a local kennel breeder, or veterinarian might be the answer.

Make sure that the female is healthy before the mating takes place. Get all her shots updated and have the veterinarian give her a complete physical to determine if she is capable of carrying a healthy litter of pups.

Once again, do not breed a bitch that is too old (over seven years of age) unless she is very healthy and very young for her age. Do the groundwork of searching for a partner before the bitch comes into season: do not wait until it is time to breed. Before the mating, all terms should be spelled out clearly and signed by both parties in order to avoid any disputes that may arise later through a change of mind by one of the parties involved. The owner of the stud will charge a set fee or take a pup (either the pick of the litter or the second pick), depending on the agreement. Some stud owners will wait until they are certain that the bitch is pregnant before receiving payment, while others demand immediate payment. If the bitch does not conceive, the right to another mating at the next season is usually granted. The agreement should also include the age at which the puppy will be picked, if applicable, and also what to do if only one puppy is born—to whom will it go? Although rare, this does happen occasionally if the mating takes place too late in the bitch's season, when only one egg is left to be fertilized.

Experienced breeder Donna LaQuatra assists her dogs throughout the entire mating.

Do not assume that the bitch will become pregnant just because she allows the mate to mount her, since most females will allow the male to mount too early and also too late in the season.

The fertile period lasts for about three to eight days depending on the bitch, usually between the 10th and 15th days of the heat. The pair should be placed together as early as the fifth day just in case the bitch is an early breeder. If they breed, wait a day and breed again. Skip a day and breed once more. They should be bred two or three times to ensure a successful mating.

PREGNANCY

An early sign of pregnancy is when, a day or so after the mating, you try to put the bitch back in with the male and she

One of the most visible (though later) signs of pregnancy is the swelling of the breasts.

The expectant mother must be kept calm and comfortable in the whelping box.

growls at him. This means that she is either pregnant or out of season. Other signs of pregnancy are: a loss or increase of appetite, growling at other dogs (especially those who are playmates), vomiting, weight gain, morning sickness, and milk in the breasts.

Around the fifth week of pregnancy, the bitch will begin to look pregnant; her sides will fill out and her breasts will begin to enlarge with milk. Gestation, or length of pregnancy, will last from 58–63 days. To determine the delivery date, count from the last mating to the 60th day. However, expect the pups on the 58th day or earlier even though they may not arrive until the 63rd day or after. You should be prepared one week in advance, with the whelping box ready and all the supplies on hand in case of an early delivery.

FEEDING DURING PREGNANCY

Feed vitamins daily with the bitch's meals from the first mating on, to be sure that she is receiving the proper nutrients. Assume that she is pregnant and feed her accordingly—extra calcium tablets and vitamin E—to ensure that she does not develop eclampsia (a condition resulting from lack of calcium in the body after birth) or have problems whelping. Vitamin E we believe will make her more elastic and thereby aid in the delivery of the pups.

The bitch should be fed about one-third more food than usual during her pregnancy. Add plenty of milk and cheese to her diet. Her appetite will begin to deteriorate near the end of the pregnancy; therefore, she will need to be fed smaller meals with extra

This new mother enjoys a high-calcium, high-protein treat of cottage cheese after completing the hard work of delivery.

snacks between meals.

If the female is overweight, feed her as usual for the first month and add just a little bit more near the end of her pregnancy. (A weight problem will cause a difficult whelping.)

few weeks of life, a whelping box is used. A whelping box can be purchased at your local pet shop or constructed from plywood and two-by-fours. The rule of thumb, however, is to buy, not build. Whatever you can make

In addition to the whelping box, many breeders provide a separate puppy box when the litter becomes more mobile.

THE WHELPING BOX

To give the bitch a place to have her pups and to care for them for the first

can usually be purchased for less. The products available for sale are designed for the expressed purpose and most always have years of experience behind them.

If you do choose to build, the size is up to the builder

and the amount of space available in the home; however, it must be large enough for the bitch to stretch out in and walk around without harming the pups. An average-sized box for a Rottweiler is approximately 3.5 by 4.5 feet and 1.25 feet in height. At such a height, the puppies will be kept from climbing out of the box too early (at least until they reach four or five weeks of age). Some breeders construct a lower box with an addition to be put on later when the puppies get older.

LABOR

There are some visible signs to let you know when the big event is close at hand. First, the bitch will begin digging holes and building a nest outside or even in your bed. Then she will start picking at her food a few days in advance of labor—typically rejecting food entirely the day the puppies are born. She will desire constant companionship and follow you around everywhere, not letting you out of her sight. As delivery nears, she will start panting heavily and may get very jumpy and impatient. She will become confused and not know whether she wants to walk around or lie down. Then she will begin whimpering and seem very agitated and restless. Next her water will break. A stringy, milky, slightly tinged discharge will be visible. She will begin turning and looking at her rear.

To help the bitch during labor, keep a bowl of fresh water close by so she can wet her mouth; she will be dry from all the panting. If necessary, put up a high board to keep her from jumping out of the box and delivering the puppies all over the house. (They do it— believe me!) Some bitches like to walk all over the place when delivering and will jump over a three-foot board to get out and have the puppies on the carpet.

Here the tail is being docked on a young Rottweiler pup.

WHELPING

You should be prepared to deliver the pups about one week before the bitch's due date just in case you have miscalculated or she delivers early. If you do not feel that you are ready to deliver puppies, you may be able to have her whelp at the veterinarian's office or find a breeder to assist you, but such arrangements should be made *prior* to the due date! It is helpful to let your vet know ahead of time when your bitch is due so that he can arrange to be available in the case of an emergency.

Here is a list of supplies that you should have on hand for delivery:

• Clean towels, washcloths, paper towels
• Blankets, indoor/outdoor carpeting
• Diapers (optional)
• Blunt scissors
• Alcohol
• Rectal thermometer
• Iodine
• Flashlight

- Red heat lamp
- Thread
- Syringe
- Newspapers
- Whelping box
- Baby bottles and formula.

SIGNS OF TROUBLE

If the mother's water breaks and she does not deliver a puppy within two to three hours, or, if she goes into labor and does not deliver a pup within three to four hours, call a vet immediately. If she becomes obviously distressed and shows this by running around and/or yelping, the puppy is most likely too large or somehow stuck in the canal; again, call a vet.

In an absolute emergency, and *only* as a last resort, you can try to help her by first washing your hands, then placing one hand into the vulva, waiting for a contraction,

After the tail is removed, a stitch can be set to limit the bleeding. Then a styptic powder can be dabbed on the incision.

turning the puppy counter-clockwise and slowly pulling him out. If he does not come out by the end of the contraction, *wait* for another contraction before continuing. If the puppy still will not come out, then it is probably too large for the mother and her life is in serious danger; a vet must be found immediately. It must be emphasized that this is an extremely delicate procedure that should be performed only by a trained expert. It is mentioned here because of its importance and as a topic that a concerned breeder may wish to research.

ASSISTING WITH THE DELIVERY

To prepare the whelping box, lay newspapers down first. Then place some blankets or indoor/outdoor carpeting in the box for the delivery. Blankets or carpeting will give the pups more footing so that you will not have "swimmers."

During the late stages of labor, stay nearby and

Here a dewclaw is being removed by clamping and scraping the thumbnail down the side of the paw. This method is very neat and less painful to the puppy.

comfort the bitch. Pat her head and give her ice or cold water to aid her dry mouth. Set up the red heat lamp about three to four feet above the whelping box to keep the puppies warm during their first two weeks of life. The red lamp will warm them but will not hurt their eyes as would a white lamp.

Stay present for the entire whelping if possible, because pups delivered without a breeder nearby are the ones most likely not to survive. The bitch can roll on one by accident or not remove the sac in time. If she does not remove the sac, it must be taken off by the breeder within 30 seconds or the pup will suffocate. To remove the sac, slip it off starting from the back, moving up over the nose (it usually slides right off after you get it started).

It is best to remove the dewclaws as soon as possible to keep the pain factor to a minimum.

HELPING A PUPPY BREATHE

After you remove the sac, the mucus must be removed from the mouth and nose. You can try a baby syringe to remove the excess or you can use the "sling-the-puppy" method. To sling the puppy, you take the puppy in one hand, place two fingers on either side of his head and one on the back of the neck to support his head and to prevent breaking his neck. Place your thumb inside the mouth to hold it open. Keeping your finger on the back of the neck and holding the other hand under the pup, sling the pup downward, stopping when his nose faces the floor. This will force the "water" out of the mouth and nose. Continue slinging until *all* the mucus has been removed.

After removing the mucus, check to see if the pup begins breathing on his own. If not, then you will have to try stimulating him. Rub the sides back and forth, up and down; this should start the pup's breathing. If he still does not begin breathing, lay him gently on your lap, place your mouth over his mouth and nostrils, and puff gently until his chest expands. Do not breathe forcefully or his lungs may burst. Let him exhale and continue until he starts coughing or whimpering.

As the bitch whelps each pup, watch to make sure that all the afterbirths are delivered, since a retained placenta could cause a serious infection. If she chooses to eat the afterbirth, let her; it will stimulate her contractions and bring on the milk.

The mother should, by instinct, chew or shred the cord from the puppy. If she does not, you will need a pair of blunt scissors to cut the cord. If the cord is cut too cleanly with sharp scissors or too close to the pup's navel, it may not stop bleeding. This is why blunt scissors should be used, and they should be

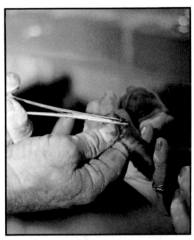

The A.K.C. standard for the breed states, "No dewclaws."

sterilized in alcohol ahead of time. To clamp or pinch the cord on the pup, pinch it or tie a piece of thread around it; dab some iodine on the end of the cord to help it dry faster.

After each pup is born, you may change some of the blanket bedding and papers or carpeting to aid the bitch and to keep the puppies warm and dry. Use a lamp to warm them and prevent any type of chill because most pups this young will die if they experience a temperature shock. Maintain a moderate temperature of 85 to 90°F (29–32°C) for the first two weeks in the whelping box.

Some breeders use disposable diapers to increase the sanitary conditions of the delivery, placing a diaper under the vulva. After the afterbirth is delivered, if the bitch does not want to eat it, it can be easily removed without too much mess. Of course, it is not always that simple to get a bitch to lie down and let you deliver the pups in this manner, but it may be worth a try.

During their first two weeks of life, the pups are completely dependent upon their mom and breeder.

Weaning time marks a special period in the growth and development of the pups; it usually begins after the third week of life.

You should place the puppies in a warm basket nearby while the bitch is still whelping—if she will let you. Some bitches prefer to keep their pups with them until the next pup is delivered. In this case, the pups will have to be moved to an outer corner where the bitch cannot accidentally step on them.

If you notice the mother's milk to be stringy, odd-colored, foul-smelling, or in any way suggesting an abnormality, do not let the pups nurse because it can poison them. Begin bottle-feeding immediately and continue until a veterinarian checks the milk and the bitch.

POSTPARTUM CARE

Within 24 hours after the delivery, the female should be checked by your veterinarian to make certain that there is not a retained puppy or any afterbirth left inside her. He will give her

a shot to clear the uterus and also a shot of penicillin to prevent infection.

DIFFICULTIES AND COMPLICATIONS

A Caesarean section is performed at the veterinary hospital when the bitch is in labor too long and does not deliver or when a pup is too

Even when they are just a few hours old, the pups should be frisky and nurse hungrily.

large to pass through the birth canal.

Eclampsia is a condition that results when the calcium level in the body drops very low, causing the female to become almost hysterical, shake uncontrollably, be very frightened, and possibly die if she does not receive an adequate amount of calcium soon—by way of supplements and cheeses, an intravenous, or even a shot if necessary. A vet will prefer not to give a shot of calcium because it will harden under the skin and cause much pain in that spot.

Mastitis is a problem in which the breasts become infected. Keep the affected area clean and drain the pus often. Set the bitch away from the pups from time to time to allow the area to be aired without the bandage. Before rebandaging it, you should apply an antibiotic ointment.

Uterine infection occurs when the uterus is not cleared out after the

delivery of such as a retained afterbirth or puppy. The bitch will become deathly ill, have a very high temperature, stop eating, and lose interest in her

Mother dogs seem to display a special pride of their first born.

pups. She will be too weak to care for them. Get her to the vet and on an antibiotic immediately. Most professional breeders give all their bitches antibiotic shots or tablets after every

The dam may become excited during the delivery process, but nonetheless she must be made to settle down and nurse her litter.

whelping to ensure that an infection like this does not develop because it can swiftly kill a mother.

Hysterectomies are sometimes necessary after a bitch gives birth if she does not stop bleeding, begins hemorrhaging, or has problems due to age, etc.

EARLY CARE FOR THE ROTTWEILER PUP

It is very important, especially during the first few days, to watch closely to make sure that all the pups are nursing. The weaker pups (the runts) will have problems competing with the larger pups to nurse. The ones not eating will begin lying very still, looking sickly, and not responding as quickly as the others when stimulated by stroking or touching of their feet. When this occurs, place them at a small nipple towards the rear of the mother, where they may have a chance to nurse. If they still have no strength to nurse or continue to be knocked away by the "chow-hounds," then they must be bottlefed or they will die from starvation.

The mother will instinctively clean the puppies. The bitch will need help keeping the whelping box clean, especially with a large litter. If the bitch is not present, the breeder should keep the puppies clean at all times.

Weaning occurs during a period of puppy development known as the litter socialization phase, and to watch the puppies feed at this age is truly delightful.

BOTTLEFEEDING

It is strongly recommended that products specially designed for puppies (bottles, nipples, formula, etc.) be used to bottlefeed a puppy. However, a small baby bottle and formula (puppy or baby formula) or a mixture of one-part evaporated milk to one-part water can be used if necessary. Open the pup's mouth and place the nipple fully into it. The pup should begin sucking on it instinctively. If he does not, hold the bottle over the pup's mouth and squeeze a little milk into his mouth. The pup will be forced to swallow. If the pup is healthy, this will be the only impetus necessary. If the pup is sick, then he will continue to have problems sucking and swallowing. Sometimes pups are born with a hole in the throat or the top of the mouth that will prevent them from nursing properly—it may take a couple of days to figure this out.

I bottlefed one pup who nursed fine for three days and then, the next feeding time, I found him cold and near death. When he tried to drink from the bottle he choked, rolled over, and died. I wrapped him loosely in a towel and thought about taking him to the vet to find out the reason for his death just in case there was something serious that I should know about this litter. About 15 minutes later I heard a puppy whimpering—but it was not coming from the whelping box; it was coming from the towel I had just set in the kitchen. The puppy was alive!

I bottlefed him and he drank actively and well. I then gave him to his mother so that she could provide him with the love and compassion that he now needed. Two more times the pup drank well from the bottle, still too weak to nurse from his mother. But then, the next time I looked into the box, he was dead. I left him there for a little

The pups should first be wormed at ten days of age, then once a week until the age of six weeks—always, of course, under the guidance and supervision of a professional.

while to make sure that he was not going to come back to life again. This time he did not. Apparently he had a breathing problem that originated in his lungs. It inhibited his intake of air and caused him to choke and die. This story shows that bottlefed pups sometimes survive with great reward to the breeder but other times are lost due to physical malformations and malfunctions, rather

Deborah Gilman's young Rotties enjoy the warm sunshine. Photo by I. Francais.

than to lack of care on your part.

TAILS AND DEWCLAWS

At three or four days of age, the tails should be docked and dewclaws should be removed—the younger the better. Every day the process is delayed, the pups grow and develop. Consequently, the procedure may become a painful experience, especially since anesthesia is not used.

We have the dewclaws removed and the tails docked at two days of age. At this early stage, the dewclaws are so small that they can be scraped right off the claw with a thumbnail. After clamping the claw and scraping the thumbnail straight down the side of the paw, the dewclaw falls off painlessly. This procedure does not leave a mark or bleed as much as when the claw is clipped away. It is very neat and simple.

After the tail is clipped (docked), a stitch may be set to ease any flow of blood that may occur. An antibiotic should then be dabbed on to prevent infection. Docking should

The pup's toenails will need to be clipped to prevent their scratching the mother. Be very careful not to cut the quick.

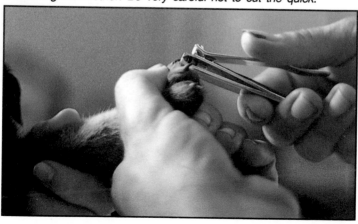

Children invariably will want to help out with the babies, and bottlefeeding is a positive way for the children to assist. Parents should always keep a watchful eye.

be performed by a veterinarian.

KEEPING RECORDS

Thorough records concerning health are important to you and the people who buy your puppies. Begin keeping track of weight and worming medications from the day of birth and continue to do so until the pup leaves for his new home. Your veterinarian can provide for you health forms to use for each pup. Many of the dog food companies will send them out with puppy packets. Keeping good records ensures that each pup receives all of his shots and other necessary care so that there will be no misunderstanding of what the dog has received: it will all be on his record.

Pups can be identified with color-coded collars from birth. Note any problems or difficulties with each pup, since such information has proven to be a valuable tool when breeding the pups in the future. Birth information can give breeders more insight into a particular dog.

As a rule applied under Section 2 of the *American Kennel Club Regulations for Registration and Show*, a breeder is required to keep accurate records for five years. The AKC now sends owners a form called "Record of a Litter Produced By:" in each litter kit sent out. It takes about three weeks to receive this kit, so breeders should send for it before the pups are born. As soon as the pups are born, the registration forms should be filled out and sent to the national organization, as this also takes about three to four weeks to process. This way, if there is a problem with any pup's name, you will have time to correct it without delaying finding a home for the pup. To send for a litter registration, write to: The American Kennel Club, 51 Madison Avenue, New York, New York 10010; or The Kennel Club of Great

Britain, 1 Clarges Street, Piccadilly, London, W1Y 8AB.

If you are going to get the pup's pedigree, you need to allow three to four weeks for that as well. Most people will want to see the pedigree before purchasing a puppy, so you should have it by the time the pups are six to eight weeks of age. There are some independent pedigree services that will get a pedigree out to you by express mail if necessary.

The owner should get copies of the pedigree, the registration papers, and the health records, as well as instructions on care and feeding.

Young Rottweilers are said to resemble little bears—and have appetites to match!

FEEDING THE PUPS

By two weeks of age, you can start introducing the pups to food in a dish. They may not understand what to do with it at first, but by the third week they will be eating like champions. The first food should be a mixture of rice cereal (baby food), plain yogurt, and evaporated milk.

Warm the milk mixture before feeding the pups; set it down in the middle of the whelping box and place the pups all around it. They will probably need some assistance to understand what to do. Gently put their mouths to the food. Their noses may get covered with the mixture, but eventually they will lick their lips and taste the flavor. Some may even catch on right away and start lapping up the mixture; others may take a few more introductions before they eat well. When

You can really note the pups' individual personalities as they interact at the feeding dishes.

The birthing of the puppies is just the beginning of the hard-earned rewards of responsible breeding.

a pup does catch on, he will dive feet first into the food dish in a zealous attempt to lap up the meal. The pups will often finish the meal and begin to whimper—this is because they have sticky stuff all over themselves which they cannot get off. Eventually they will huddle together and lick each other clean. If they do not, it is wise to wipe the pups clean with a warm damp cloth.

Feed the pups four times a day between feedings from their mother. Slowly build up the meals by adding a bit more food each day. When the pups reach four weeks of age, introduce them to puppy food. You can give it sooner (at three weeks) if you let it sit in hot water for a while and then add some of it to the rice and yogurt mixture. Let it stand until it is a soft mash, and then give it to the pups. You will notice a difference in the pups' stools soon after they begin eating dog food. As the pups grow, you will need to increase the number of feeding dishes.

SPECIAL CARE FOR THE PUPS

Puppies are extremely susceptible to disease and illness—germs of all kinds attack the pups incessantly. A routine vaccination schedule started at six weeks of age and continued until all shots are given will help protect your pups from illness. There is usually a six, an eight, a ten, and a twelve-week shot to be given. Distemper, parvo, and rabies shots will have to be done every year or every two years depending on the type of shot given to the dog.

Kennel cough is very contagious, especially to young pups. A veterinarian can administer drops in the pup's nose to prevent this illness. This would be wise if you are planning to take your troops to a dog show or training class, for there they will be more likely to come into contact with an infected or carrier dog.

It is best to keep the young pups away from other animals, especially stray dogs. It is also wise to keep visitors to a minimum until the pups are older and their immune systems more effective. Germs can be passed from a child's hand to the pup through a simple petting. If a single pup is infected, there is a great likelihood that the disease will spread through the litter.

Going to the vet's office also presents the danger of bacterial and viral infection. Ask your vet if it is at all possible for him to come outside to your vehicle or to schedule an early morning appointment so as to avoid contact with any sick animal.

PARASITE CONTROL

At about two weeks of age, fleas begin to become a problem to puppies. Naturally, you do not want to bathe them at this early age. You can, however, rub them with a mild flea spray. This will not harm them if you are careful not to get it around their eyes or noses, for the alcohol could irritate them. To give the pup a rubdown, spray a small

The pup must feel secure when being held, otherwise it may wriggle and even attempt to jump down. Photo by I. Francais of pup owned by Robert Sarro.

amount of the flea preparation on a cloth, wrap the cloth around the pup, and hold the cloth in place for a few moments. This should kill all the fleas in the covered area. A flea mat, which is made of bay leaves, cedar chips, and cedar oil, will also help to keep fleas under control. A flea mat can be purchased at your local pet shop.

If necessary, when your pups reach the age of five or six weeks, you can

Every new owner must be thoroughly educated to the breed—including its growth rate. This Rottie pup will soon be more than an armful.

experience the "joy" of giving them their first flea bath. When bathing the pups, never use any harsh chemicals. You can use a mild bath oil to help repel fleas and give the coat a beautiful sheen.

INFORMING THE NEW OWNER

Not all puppy buyers know how to care for their new pet. Some buyers will know from experience; but, as the breeder, you are responsible to take time to explain how you have cared for the pup. This includes which food the puppy has been eating, how much he should be fed and at what intervals, and any other information that would be useful to the new owner. (You would be surprised at how many people think that all dogs, regardless of age, should eat only one meal a day.)

It is always better to prepare a list of items to cover with new owners because it is too easy to forget something when they arrive. Some breeders prepare a checklist and make copies to give to the new owners along with the health records and registration papers. This is a nice thought, especially for people who easily forget things once they leave your home. In this way they can refer back to the list to refresh their memory. Also, as a breeder, you must keep good records for the national kennel club by recording the name, address, and phone number of each buyer. By doing so you can also do follow-up checks to see how the pups are doing in their new homes. Most good breeders keep track of all their dogs in this manner. It is surprising how many kennel owners can actually remember a vast number of puppy names. I know one breeder who knows the names of all the dogs she has bred and all the owners to which these dogs went. Amazing! Yet she somehow mixes up her children's names all the

Children and puppies can be mutually beneficial to each other's growing up.

time...I guess we all have our foibles.

FINDING HOMES FOR THE PUPS

Some breeders use what they call a "seller's contract" when they sell a pup. This contract helps ensure the safety and proper care of the dog in the new home. These contracts may state that the new owner promises to give the dog proper veterinary care; will breed the dog only to a champion or other suitable dog of the same breed; will not sell to a new home without the kennel owners being notified. The items mentioned here are just a few general concerns which may be found in the document. It is not uncommon for a seller's contract to be drawn up by a lawyer and to be very in-depth. The most important

Puppies have times of great exuberance and energy, but they tire quickly and need plenty of rest.

concern of any seller's contract must be the best interests of the breed. (Some breeders do not use a contract but merely ask the buyer to give first option if they ever decide to sell the dog.) If you are interested in reviewing a standard breeder's contract, blank contracts are available from most breed registries.

PUPPY CHARADES

Contrary to common belief, puppies do not sleep all the time. No matter how few puppies there are, and no matter how many nipples there are, two or three pups will always fight over one nipple. The pups will push and shove each other off in a furious attempt to win the nipple—and so begins the ongoing activity of sibling rivalry.

Some pups will begin to show their personalities as early as 11 days after birth. There will be the agitator who barks and yelps, the sleeper who does not care what is going on around

At just a few weeks of age, each pup will have its own identity, and every family member may well have a favorite.

him, the runt who is feisty and quick, the eater who is the fattest one and who wears the evidence of his "hoggedness," and, of course, there will be others whom you can quickly distinguish by their own behavioral characteristics.

By two weeks of age, the eyes slowly begin to open and the pups soon learn how to walk on shaky, wobbly legs. At first, however, the pups scoot around by pulling themselves by their forepaws. With a little practice, they soon are up and at'em. Once they learn to walk, they soon learn how to run. They are apt to charge the first person on sight in an incessant quest for food.

Wrestling among the pups begins at about two-and-a-half weeks of age along with rolling and tumbling, playful biting, barking, growling, and other amusing antics. Also, at this age, the pups' eyes are fully open. They will now look to you when you call them. They are more aware of their surroundings and are especially aware when mother is not in the box.

At three weeks of age, running is the norm of locomotion. When mom gets in the box, it is usually cause for a major fiasco. She must dodge back and forth just to find a spot to settle in without stomping on a pup. The mother must then circle and circle in an attempt to lie down without sitting on a pup, which is almost impossible since all the pups run and dash in crazy circles yelping for her. The bitch will need

assistance in restraining the pups if she is to lie down. Sometimes a pup will get stuck behind the mother or get rolled up in the blankets or sheets and will need assistance to get free. If not helped, the pup could be smothered or get rolled on by the mother—keep an

eye out for such situations.
By three-and-a-half
weeks, all personalities
emerge. One is always the

*Providing the growing pup with a
Nylabone® helps to induce growth
of the permanent teeth and to get
rid of the puppy teeth on time.
Photo by R. Reagan.*

"mama's boy"—the one
who hollers and screams
when mom leaves is the
first to figure out how to
climb out of the box (and
does so often). He is also
the one who starts the
others' yelping and crying.
At four weeks of age the
puppies become especially

cute and cuddly. If you are planning on keeping one, you probably know by now which one it will be.

The runts of the litters that I have bred always turn out to be girls (a coincidence I'm sure). They are usually labeled "little one" or "baby." They are always sweet and lovable and very intelligent—as the runt of any litter is usually said to be "smart as a whip."

When mother is not in the box, the pups tend to

Like children, pups need a sense of security and consistency in their environment.

huddle together for security. If one gets separated from the bunch, he will cry out from fear and loneliness. A good sign that a pup has been separated is an ear-piercing yelp that does not cease.

At four or five weeks of age, the pups begin teething, so mom will probably not want to bother with nursing them any more. She will start weaning them on her own and leaving them on their own for progressively longer periods of time. The mother may even need to be forced to spend time with the pups because she so dislikes their attack on her nipples with their new teeth. At this time, water bowls should be provided for the pups at all times, and the amount of food given should be increased. If the climate is mild, you may also wish to build a pen of some sort for them to spend some of the day outside. You must, however, bring them in for the night.

PREPARING THE PUPS FOR THE WORLD

It is important to work with your pups every day, or every other day at least, after they reach the age of six weeks. If they are just left outside in a pen until someone comes along to buy one of them, there could be serious consequences. For example, they many come hard to reverse); or they could become very timid or lose that natural Rottweiler ability to protect and guard.

To prepare your Rottie pups for the world, let them run and play with each other, with children, and with adults. The pups love to play with kids, and kids love to play with puppies;

Much of the dog's view of man comes from his puppyhood relationships with him. Photo by I. Francais.

to fear people; they may develop inferiority complexes (which are very but watch them carefully because small children, and even some teens, do not know how to handle dogs and, without realizing it, can hurt them. Toddlers like to pick puppies up by the neck and carry them around which could strangle them.

When the pups bark at strangers, reward them with a pat on the head or a hug and say "Good dog," and tell them "It's OK," if the stranger is of no concern. It is very important for the pups to be around their mother to see her act out the dog role in the family, a role which they will quickly learn by observation. The mother can teach the pups how to protect and guard their territory if you simply allow them to watch her in action.

I cannot emphasize enough the need to exercise the pups. If they are kept in a large pen area where they can run and play, the need is not as great; but, if they are kept in a small pen, they should be let out to run and stretch their legs at least a couple of hours each day. The problem with too little exercise is that it creates a pup that is very wild, unruly, and hard to train. He will get to a point where he will not listen to anyone if cramped up too long in a small pen. Then when someone comes to pet him, he will be too wild and thereby prove undesirable. It may come to the point where no one will want him because of his wildness, and soon he will face the brunt of constant rejection and become even more wild in an attempt to capture someone's attention. He does not understand that the wild behavior is what is turning the people away; he is merely trying hard to get someone's love and affection in the only way he knows.

If possible, get the pups used to a leash. Take one pup out at a time; put the leash on him and let him wander around with you following; then pick up the end and try to walk him around the yard. At first he will buck and squirm like a wild pony, but after a few introductions he will master walking on a leash and will soon look forward to your special training sessions.

The dam's role is that of pack leader. She has the greatest environmental influence on the litter's early social development. Photo by I. Francais.

Another experience where puppies learn control is the bath. Keep telling them to stay and settle down while you wash each one individually. This way they are introduced to yet another command and they begin to understand.

While the pups are young it is easy to teach the "Come" command, since every time you call them they run to you. Let the pups out and call each one separately by clapping your hands or getting down on all fours and clapping the ground at their eye level. When they run to you, praise them and say "Good dog."

The more you work with the pups, the nicer their personalities and the better their chances of a happy homelife in their new environment will be. Teach them the fundamental commands such as: "No," "Come," "Go out," "No bark," etc. The more you talk to the puppies and teach them to respect commands, the more obedient the pups will be before leaving for their new homes.

A very notable breeder, Helen Jones, once told me a valuable piece of puppy psychology that I feel is good advice to pass on: "Treat your puppy like a stupid puppy and you will have a stupid puppy. But if you expect him to understand Master's language, then he will do so. The puppy is what you make him." This summarizes in a nutshell what I have been explaining

so far in this chapter: the pups look up to you, they love you and want to be everything for you; therefore, do not chain the pup, ignore him, or yell and scream abusive threats, because you will break his spirit and character for life. You must have an amount of compassion and understanding to raise dogs. If you do not have the patience and time, dog breeding is not for you.

Everything you teach your pups before they leave home will make coping with life in the strange world just a little bit easier. Picture yourself as the puppy. You leave your familiar home, your mother, and your loved ones behind to go to this strange place. Everyone is unknown and they do everything differently than back home. At least when he hears those familiar words or has a familiar toy that you have sent with him, he will have something to make him feel a little at ease.

The distinguished Ch. Delphi Thetis Von BeaBear, owned by Donna LaQuatra, taking Group First. Photo by Meyer.

Donna LaQuatra was Top Breeder of the year in 1986. Like most other dog show enthusiasts, Donna caught the bug (the show bug that is) after her very first show at the Ocala Dog Club in 1979. "I loved it! I was so

thrilled!" is how she expressed the feeling of the moment. From there she continued on and in 1986, she tied with Jeanne Jackson from Tennessee for Breeder of the Year. To a serious breeder, nothing could be more flattering than to receive such an award.

Residing in High Springs, Florida, Donna puts all her

efforts into her family and her business, the well-known BeaBear Rottweiler Kennels. To add to her list of accomplishments, Donna has 11 champions to her credit. Some of Donna's well-known champions are: Ch. Delphi Thetis Von BeaBear, ranked No. 1 Working Group Bitch in 1985, No. 2 Breed Bitch for 1985, and No. 4 Working Group and Breed Bitch for 1986; Ch. RC's Lexia Von Ursa, TT, ranked No. 2 Top Producer for 1985 and 1986; and Ch. BeaBear Von Shadow, ranked No. 4 Working Group and No. 9 Breed for 1981.

In an intensive study, Donna taught herself to show by following the top

Ch. BeaBear's Something Special, bred and owned by Donna LaQuatra, taking Best of Winners. Photo by Earl Graham Studios.

Ch. BeaBear's Donna J Von Magnum attained her championship in 1986 and thereby helped Donna LaQuatra tie for Breeder of the Year.

handlers: "I ran around the ring behind all the top people who I knew were winning; I used to sit outside the ring and study them."

When asked, "Why Rottweilers?" Donna replied, "Because they are just fantastic and I like them." Donna has had success with many other breeds as well, including Pointers (with the No. 1 Pointer in the U.S.), Pugs, and Great Danes. And while she loves these other breeds, especially the Danes, Donna knows that to improve a breed and really make strides toward the ideal dog, one must stay exclusively with one breed. Donna has chosen and is committed to the Rottweiler.

All breeders have their own way of doing things, and like most others, Donna has lived and learned by experience. The following is a list of tips and pointers that Donna felt would be most beneficial and interesting to anyone wishing to breed Rottweilers.

SELECTING A SIRE

He should be O.F.A. certified for his hips; have a scissors bite; have no missing teeth.

Check the pedigree first; then check the dog. (Donna turns a lot of people down for stud service because she does not like the pedigree.)

MATCHING PEDIGREES

Be selective! There is too much over-breeding with dogs of bad conformation.

Do research on the pedigree and never breed simply because a dog is conveniently located.

When doing research on the stud, be sure to check for all hereditary problems such as bad bite, missing teeth, etc. Donna feels that bad bites are the most prevalent problem and can be passed hereditarily.

Linebreeding should be only to grandparents (the second or third ancestors common to both dogs).

When outcrossing to phase out specific faults, have a breeder assist you, one who knows well the pedigrees and past faults of each line.

CONTRACTS

Regardless of what is stated in the contract, have it notarized; it may not otherwise hold up in court.

Many contracts vary in regard to the turnover arrangements; i.e., some people make payments and the papers are held until payment is complete, others in one lump sum.

Puppies are living beings, subject to change as they develop. When buying or selling, be sure that all guarantees and non-guarantees are clearly stated in writing. Photo by I. Francais.

There are many other possibilities as well.

Get a copy of a standard contract from the AKC or another reliable organization. These sample contracts are available for studs, puppy sales, and other specific circumstances.

If you sell a puppy without a guarantee, be sure that it is in writing.

MATING

The bitch should be taken to the male on the fifth day of heat (just in case she is an early breeder) and remain there through the 15th day.

The bitch is ready when the swelling of the vulva just starts to go down and the discharge changes from red to a lighter, pinkish color. The stud dog will usually sense this. (Some veterinarians believe that the color change is not a reliable sign of readiness; however, Donna has had only two bitches in ten years that have not changed color.)

If no change in color occurs, breed between the 10th and 15th day.

In the case of a "non-breeding," artificial insemination can be an option if both parties are in agreement.

Always breed twice: breed; skip a day; breed again.

WHELPING

Do not leave the bitch alone during this stage, especially during the first week. Donna sleeps beside the whelping box for the first three weeks after the delivery. She starts sleeping on the couch three days before the bitch is due.

The bitch can deliver up to five days early, but this is very uncommon.

A drop in the bitch's temperature is not an accurate sign that the delivery is about to begin; this is because the temperature may drop as early as a week before she is ready to deliver.

The best signs of delivery are the water breaking and a clear, stringy, milky discharge usually occurring between the 60th and 63rd day.

If the water breaks and the bitch goes for two-and-a-half hours without delivering a puppy, *call your vet!* (Donna has lost puppies because the first was not delivered on time.)

Delayed delivery could be a sign that the pup is too large, and the bitch may need a Caesarean section. C-sections can be performed only by a trained professional.

A training tip: After the dog learns to retrieve, tossing the dumbbell over the high jump can encourage him to go over.

AFTER THE BIRTH

After the birthing is complete, the bitch should be given a "cleaning-out" shot of oxytocin or other preparation recommended by your veterinarian. This should be given within three hours if at all possible; it prevents a retained placenta, which is a common complication.

To test the bitch's milk, squeeze the nipple and run the milk out over your hand. If it runs freely, it is fine. But if it is gritty, thick, stringy, or grainy, call your vet as soon as possible; he may choose to put her on antibiotics.

Bitches with a history of mastitis can be put on antibiotics about one week prior to delivery to be continued through the first week of nursing to prevent infection—but only under the advice of a veterinarian.

A mammary discharge that is green and foul smelling is cause for great concern and must be rectified immediately.

If the bitch is not eating,

you may try boiled and strained ground beef mixed with her usual food.

The two most common problems are bad milk and the bitch's stepping on the puppies. With care and consideration, these problems can be minimized.

IMMEDIATE CARE FOR THE PUPS

Have your bitch lie down and remain as still as possible while you remove all the puppies from the box. Put them in a safe basket or box with a heating pad and cover the box with a towel to prevent chill—allowing for air flow, however. Then let the bitch get up, stretch her limbs, and relieve herself if she wishes. Afterwards, put her back into the box first and the pups second to prevent any of the pups from getting stepped on. This procedure can be repeated any time the bitch needs a little exercise.

For the first 24 hours, make sure that each of the pups is getting a nipple. If not, nurse a nipple into one's mouth. During the first 24 hours, the pups receive colostrum from the mother; this first milk secreted will help to combat disease. (If the pups do not receive colostrum, they may develop complications later on.)

WEANING

At two-and-a-half weeks, start feeding the puppies "mush" about three to four times a day. (Donna uses a quality puppy food mixed with a milk formula, adds some quality canned puppy food or strained baby meats, and adds some warm water for moisture.) This "mush" should be of a consistency that allows the pups to lap it up easily.

Have the pups completely weaned by five weeks of age.

SHOTS

Shots are very important to protect against the many canine diseases floating around. Your vet will know which shots are necessary

This page: *Schutzhund or attack training is no longer favored for Rottweilers as the breed is naturally protective and intensely strong.*

and at what time they should be given. Your vet is a trained professional. Work with him/her and all should go well. Contact your vet prior to your decision to breed and keep in close correspondence throughout the breeding and weaning process.

PUPPIES SOLD AS PETS

In some cases, pups sold as pets should go without papers, e.g., the pup is

In addition to knowing your breeding dog's genetics, you must also know his performance potential.

healthy but not a good representation of the breed. With or without papers, never sell an unhealthy or problem-ridden pup—this will only damage the breed and cause misery to the pup and purchaser involved.

A bitch sold without

Top and Bottom: *When Donna trains a dog to jump, she first lays the boards on the ground for the dog to go over. When it's time for the real thing, her training partner encourages the dog to jump over while Donna works the lead.*

papers should be spayed immediately after her first heat; this should be in the sales contract. Indeed, any animal that is sold without papers, with obvious conformational deviations, or with health or disposition problems should be spayed or neutered by a veterinarian.

INDEX

Index

SUGGESTED READING

If you wish to continue your study of breeding, the dog world and of course the Rottweiler, here are some additional books from T.F.H. to aid you in your research. All titles are available at your local pet shop, book seller or directly from the publisher.

DOG BREEDING FOR PROFESSIONALS
by Dr. Herbert Richards
TFH H-969
Hardcover, 5 1/2 x 8", 224 pages;
105 black and white photographs;
62 color photos; 4 charts.

THE ATLAS OF DOG BREEDS OF THE WORLD
by Bonnie Wilcox, DVM, and Chris Walkowicz
TFH H-1091
Hardcover, 9 1/2 x 12 1/2", 912 pages;
Over 1100 full-color photos and drawings.

THE MINI-ATLAS OF DOG BREEDS
by Andrew De Prisco and James B. Johnson
TFH H-1106
Hardcover, 5 1/2x 8 1/2"
544 pages.

THE CANINE LEXICON
by Andrew De Prisco and James B. Johnson
TFH TS-175
Hardcover
896 pages;
Over 1,300 full-color photographs.

PIT BULLS AND TENACIOUS GUARD DOGS
by Dr. Carl Semencic
TFH TS-141
Hardcover, 7 x 10", 300 pages;
Over 300 full-color photos and drawings.

THE BOOK OF THE ROTTWEILER
by Anna Katherine Nicholas
TFH H-1035
Hardcover, 5 1/2 x 8" 544 pages;
89 full-color photos and 378 black and white photos.

THE WORLD OF ROTTWEILERS
by Anna Katherine Nicholas
TFH H-1083
Hardcover, 8 1/2 x 11", 336 pages;
583 full-color photos, 79 black and white photos; 86 line drawings.

THE PROFESSIONAL'S BOOK OF ROTTWEILERS
by Anna Katherine Nicholas
TFH TS-147
Hardcover, 8 1/2 x 11", 446 pages;
Over 700 full-color photos.

THE ROTTWEILER
by Richard F. Stratton
TFH PS-820
Hardcover, 6 x 9", 256 pages;
Over 100 full-color and black and white photos

KW-229
Breeding Rottweilers